Y0-CPE-754

PORTRAITS OF THE STATES

MARYLAND

by Jonatha A. Brown

Please visit our web site at: www.garethstevens.com
For a free color catalog describing Gareth Stevens Publishing's list of high-quality books and multimedia programs, call 1-800-542-2595 (USA) or 1-800-387-3178 (Canada). Gareth Stevens Publishing's fax: (877) 542-2596.

Library of Congress Cataloging-in-Publication Data

Brown, Jonatha A.
Maryland / Jonatha A. Brown.
p. cm. — (Portraits of the states)
Includes bibliographical references and index.
ISBN-10: 0-8368-4668-0 ISBN-13: 978-0-8368-4668-3 (lib. bdg.)
ISBN 0-8368-4687-7 ISBN-13: 978-0-8368-4687-4 (softcover)
1. Maryland—Juvenile literature. I. Title. II. Series.
F181.3.B755 2006
975.2—dc22 2005044478

Updated edition reprinted in 2007. First published in 2006 by
Gareth Stevens Publishing
A Weekly Reader® Company
1 Reader's Digest Rd.
Pleasantville, NY 10570-7000 USA

Editorial direction: Mark J. Sachner
Project manager: Jonatha A. Brown
Editor: Catherine Gardner
Art direction and design: Tammy West
Picture research: Diane Laska-Swanke
Production: Jessica Morris and Robert Kraus

Picture credits: Cover, © CORBIS; pp. 4, 15, 16, 18, 24, 25 © Mae Scanlan; p. 5 © Corel; p. 6 © North Wind Picture Archives; p. 7 © Library of Congress; p. 8 © Mansell/Time & Life Pictures/Getty Images; pp. 10, 17 © MPI/Getty Images; p. 11 © PhotoDisc; p. 12 © Arthur Siegel/Getty Images; pp. 20, 26 © Pat & Chuck Blackley; pp. 22, 27 © Gibson Stock Photography; p. 28 © Don Emmert/AFP/Getty Images; p. 29 © Photo File/MLB Photos via Getty Images

Printed in the United States of America

3 4 5 6 7 8 9 10 09 08 07

CONTENTS

Words that are defined in the Glossary appear in **bold** the first time they are used in the text.

On the Cover: Baltimore's beautiful harbor is both historic and modern.

Introduction

Welcome to Maryland! Here you will find sandy beaches and a huge bay that nearly cuts the state in half. You will also find craggy mountains and sparkling rivers. Maryland is a beautiful place!

Some very famous people like to visit Maryland. U.S. presidents come here to relax. A special place in the mountains is kept up just for the president's use. Even so, you do not need to be famous to visit this state. Everyone is welcome.

So, come to Maryland! Visit its historic cities and peaceful countryside. Have a great time!

The Chesapeake Bay Bridge connects the Eastern Shore to the rest of the state.

The state flag of Maryland.

MARYLAND FACTS

- Became the 7th U.S. State: April 28, 1788
- Population (2006): 5,615,727
- Capital: Annapolis
- Biggest Cities: Baltimore, Columbia, Silver Spring, Dundalk
- Size: 9,774 square miles (25,315 square kilometers)
- Nickname: The Old Line State
- State Tree: White oak
- State Flower: Black-eyed Susan
- State Dog: Chesapeake Bay retriever
- State Bird: Baltimore oriole

History

Native Americans came to Maryland more than ten thousand years ago. They hunted, fished, and found wild plants to eat. Early Native people also grew corn, beans, and squash.

Explorers and Settlers

An Italian explorer may have sailed into Chesapeake Bay in 1524. A few Spaniards came about fifty years later. These people did not stay long. The British reached the area in 1608. They had already built a town on the coast of Virginia. Now, they were ready to settle the land farther north.

Maryland became a British **colony** in 1632. King Charles I gave the land to Cecilius Calvert, Lord Baltimore. Calvert made his brother the governor of the new

William Claiborne built a trading post on Kent Island in 1631.

IN MARYLAND'S HISTORY

Drawing the Line

In the 1700s, Pennsylvania and Maryland could not agree on their border. They argued for years. Finally, they hired Charles Mason and Jeremiah Dixon to **survey** the land. Their job was to draw a map of the border. The men finished their work in 1767. Now, the border was clear. It was named the Mason-Dixon Line after the men who mapped it.

colony. The brother brought settlers to the area two years later. The settlers bought land from the Native people. On this land, they built St. Mary's City. This city was the capital of the colony for more than sixty years.

Unsettled Times

The white settlers lived at peace with the Natives. Yet, they did not live at peace with each other. They argued over the borders of

This stone and others like it can still be seen along the Mason-Dixon Line. Mason and Dixon laid these stones as they surveyed the border between Maryland and Pennsylvania.

First Town

In 1631, William Claiborne opened a trading post on Chesapeake Bay. It was at Kent Island. This trading post became the first lasting white settlement in the area.

Up and down the East Coast, colonists fought for freedom during the Revolutionary War. Few battles were fought in Maryland, so Marylanders went to other colonies to fight.

the colony. They also argued over religion. Both Catholics and Protestants lived in the area. They did not get along. Each group wanted to be in control of the colony.

In 1649, a new law was passed. It was the Act of Religious Toleration. This law made all Christian faiths legal in Maryland. It was the first law of its kind in the British colonies.

The new law did not bring an end to the fighting. The Calverts lost control of the area twice over the next fifty years. In 1715, the king helped the Calverts get the land back again. Soon, the Calverts passed laws that took away all freedom of religion in the colony.

Fighting for Freedom

By the mid-1700s, Britain owned thirteen American

IN MARYLAND'S HISTORY

Tea Parties

In 1773, the British put a tax on tea. To **protest** this tax, settlers in some colonies destroyed shipments of tea as soon as they reached their shores. These protests were called "tea parties." Protestors in Maryland held their own tea party. When a ship full of tea sailed into the harbor at Annapolis, they burned it!

What's in a Name?

Cecilius Calvert named his colony after Queen Henrietta Maria. She was the wife of King Charles I. At first, he called the colony Terra Maria. This is Latin for "Mary's Land."

colonies. The king made the colonists pay taxes. Many of the colonists did not think these taxes were fair. They were tired of British rule, and they wanted to be free.

The Revolutionary War started in 1775. Few battles were fought in Maryland. Still, many Marylanders joined the fight. Others built cannons and ships. These people wanted to beat the British. They won the war in 1783. Five years later, Maryland became the seventh U.S. state.

Famous People of Maryland

Thurgood Marshall

Born: July 2, 1908, Baltimore, Maryland

Died: January 24, 1993, Bethesda, Maryland

Thurgood Marshall was the first African American to serve on the U.S. Supreme Court. As a younger man, he was a lawyer. He worked on **civil rights** cases. He fought against laws that were unfair to African Americans. He helped black people get the same rights as whites. In 1967, President Lyndon Johnson appointed him to the Supreme Court. He served on the court for twenty-four years.

Fighting Song

The United States and Britain went to war again in 1812. This time, Maryland was the scene of some big battles. One took place in Baltimore. Francis Scott Key watched this battle. As he watched the fight, he wrote a poem about fighting for freedom. His poem became a song called "The Star-Spangled Banner." In 1931, this song became the U.S. national anthem.

Baltimore Grows

Baltimore grew quickly in the early 1800s. It became the biggest city in the state. In the 1800s, a railroad was built to carry goods from Baltimore to other cities. Canals were dug so boats could carry cargo inland, too. Baltimore had long been a center for building ships. Now, it was also a center for trade.

Civil War

In the mid-1800s, the United States faced a big problem. Most Northern states did not allow slavery. Many people there wanted to ban slavery all over the country. People in the South kept slaves.

The battle of Antietam lasted just one day. Even so, it was one of the bloodiest battles of the Civil War.

Antietam National Battlefield is a quiet spot today.

They did not want to give them up. The two sides could not agree.

Most of the Southern states broke away from the rest of the country in 1861. They formed a new nation. It was called the Confederate States of America. Maryland is a Southern state, and some people owned slaves at that time. Even so, the state stayed in the **Union**.

The Union did not want the South to break away. Soon, the two sides began fighting the Civil War.

Maryland sided with the North. Yet some people in the state wanted to fight for the South. Those people joined the Confederate Army. Many battles were fought in Maryland.

The North won the Civil War in 1865. Then, the two countries became one again. Slavery was outlawed across the nation.

IN MARYLAND'S HISTORY

Bloody Battle

The Battle of Antietam was one of the worst battles of the Civil War. It was fought in western Maryland in 1862. More than 22,000 soldiers died in this battle. More people died that day than on any other day of the war.

During World War II, many women in Maryland worked in factories. These women helped build ships.

The Twentieth Century

In 1917, the United States entered World War I. The people of Maryland built ships and made supplies. Many businesses in the state did well during and soon after the war.

The situation changed in the 1930s. Prices fell, and factories and shops closed. Thousands of Marylanders lost their jobs. This period was known as the **Great Depression**. People all over the country had a hard time during these years.

The United States entered World War II in 1941. Once again, workers were needed in Maryland's factories. Thousands of people came to the state to work. They built ships and made guns to fight the war.

In the late 1960s, the state had problems. **Race riots** broke out in Baltimore. Not long after, factories began to move to other states. Many people in Maryland were left without jobs.

Since that time, people of all races have learned to work with each other better. High-tech companies have moved to Maryland. The city of Baltimore has fixed up its harbor area. Now, the harbor attracts tourists. The state is doing well.

Time Line

1524	The French sail into Chesapeake Bay.
1608	The English start exploring the area that is now Maryland.
1632	King Charles I gives Maryland to Lord Baltimore.
1634	Leonard Calvert and a group of British settlers found St. Mary's.
1649	The Act of Religious Toleration is passed.
1767	The Mason-Dixon Line is drawn.
1788	Maryland becomes the seventh U.S. state.
1861–1865	Maryland stays in the Union during the Civil War.
1917–1918	Maryland makes ships and supplies to help fight World War I.
1930s	The state suffers through the Great Depression.
1941-1945	Maryland provides factory jobs to many workers during World War II.
1967	Thurgood Marshall becomes the first African American to serve on the U.S. Supreme Court.
1985	Maryland begins to clean up pollution in the Chesapeake Bay.

People

Well over five million people live in Maryland. Most of the people live in cities or large towns.

Baltimore

Baltimore is the biggest city. More than 12 percent of the people in the state live there. Yet, since 1980, many people have been moving out of this city. They would rather live in the nearby towns and cities. Baltimore's leaders are now working to make their city a better place to live.

Hispanics: In the 2000 U.S. Census, 4.3 percent of the people in Maryland called themselves Latino or Hispanic. Most of them or their relatives came from places where Spanish is spoken. They may come from different racial backgrounds.

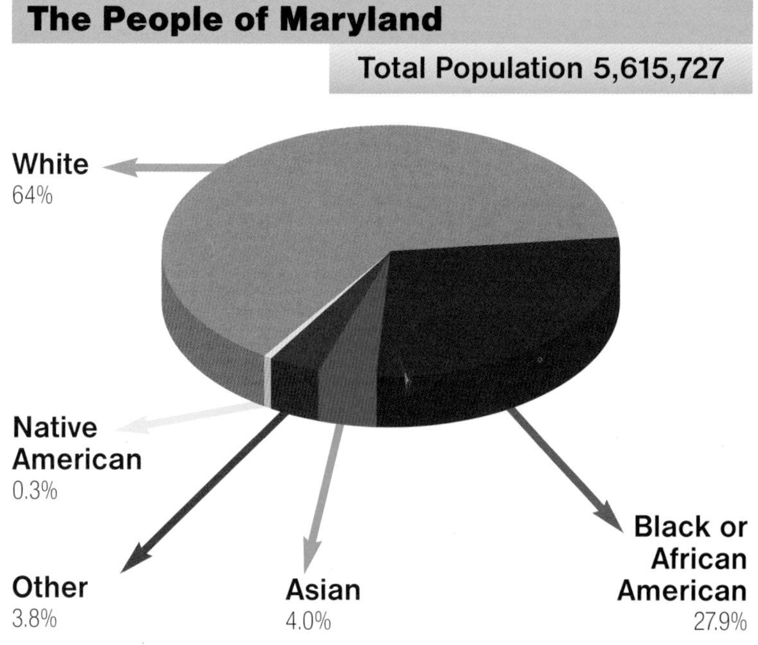

Percentages are based on the 2000 Census.

The city of Baltimore has a lovely harbor. Tourists come to the harbor to stroll, shop, and stop for a bite to eat. Many visit the city's famous aquarium.

Where People Come From

Maryland has been attracting all kinds of people for a long time. The British were the first non-Native group to settle there. In the 1800s, Baltimore became a busy entry point for **immigrants**. Ships full of Germans, Poles, and other Europeans docked in the harbor. Many of these people stayed in Baltimore and found jobs in factories. Today, about two-thirds of the people in the state have European backgrounds.

Before the Civil War, free blacks from other parts of the South came to Maryland. More free blacks lived here than in any other state. In the mid-1900s, still more African Americans moved to

This is Bancroft Hall at the U.S. Naval Academy in Annapolis. Here, men and women learn to be officers in the Navy and Marines.

the state. Today, more than one-fourth of the people in this state are African American. In Baltimore, about six in ten people are black.

People are still coming to Maryland from other parts of the world. Some are from Central America. Others are from India and Africa. Each group of people brings its own ways to the state. They make Maryland an interesting place to live.

Religion and Education

Most people in Maryland are Christian. Most of these Christians are Methodists, Catholics, and Baptists. Almost 5 percent of the people are Jewish. Hindus, Buddhists, and Muslims live here, too.

In the early years of the colony, there were few schools. The first public schools opened in 1694. Still, the state did not have a strong public school system until the early 1900s.

For a long time, black and white children went to separate schools. In 1954, the U.S. Supreme Court said this was not fair. By the

1970s, all public schools in the state served students of all races.

Maryland has many fine colleges and universities. Johns Hopkins University is well known. It is in Baltimore. The U.S. Naval Academy is also famous. It is in Annapolis. The University of Maryland has campuses in several cities.

Famous People of Maryland

Harriet Tubman

Born: About 1820, Dorchester County, Maryland

Died: March 10, 1913, Auburn, New York

Harriet Tubman was born a slave. She was put to work as a maid when she was five years old. When she grew up, she ran away. She went to Pennsylvania and became a free woman. Yet she did not forget the slaves in the South. She went back there many times. Each time, she helped more slaves run away. In all, she helped about three hundred slaves escape to freedom. During the Civil War, she was a nurse, a cook, and a spy. When the war ended, she worked for equal rights for women and African Americans.

The Land

Maryland is a southern state on the Atlantic Coast. It has hot, humid summers and mild winters.

The state is made up of two nearly separate bodies of land. Between them lies the Chesapeake Bay. On one side of the bay is the Eastern Shore. On the other side is the Western Shore. The two parts of the state meet just north of the bay.

FUN FACTS

A Special Island

Assateague Island is in the Atlantic Ocean. Most of this long, narrow island belongs to Maryland. The rest of it belongs to Virginia. A state park is in one section of the island. The rest is the Assateague Island National Seashore. Visitors can hike, bike, and watch wild ponies run on the sand.

Water, Water, and More Water

The Atlantic Ocean forms part of Maryland's eastern border. The state's coastline along the Atlantic is about 31 miles (50 km) long.

Sailboats bob at their moorings on the Susquehanna River. The Susquehanna cuts through the northeast corner of the state.

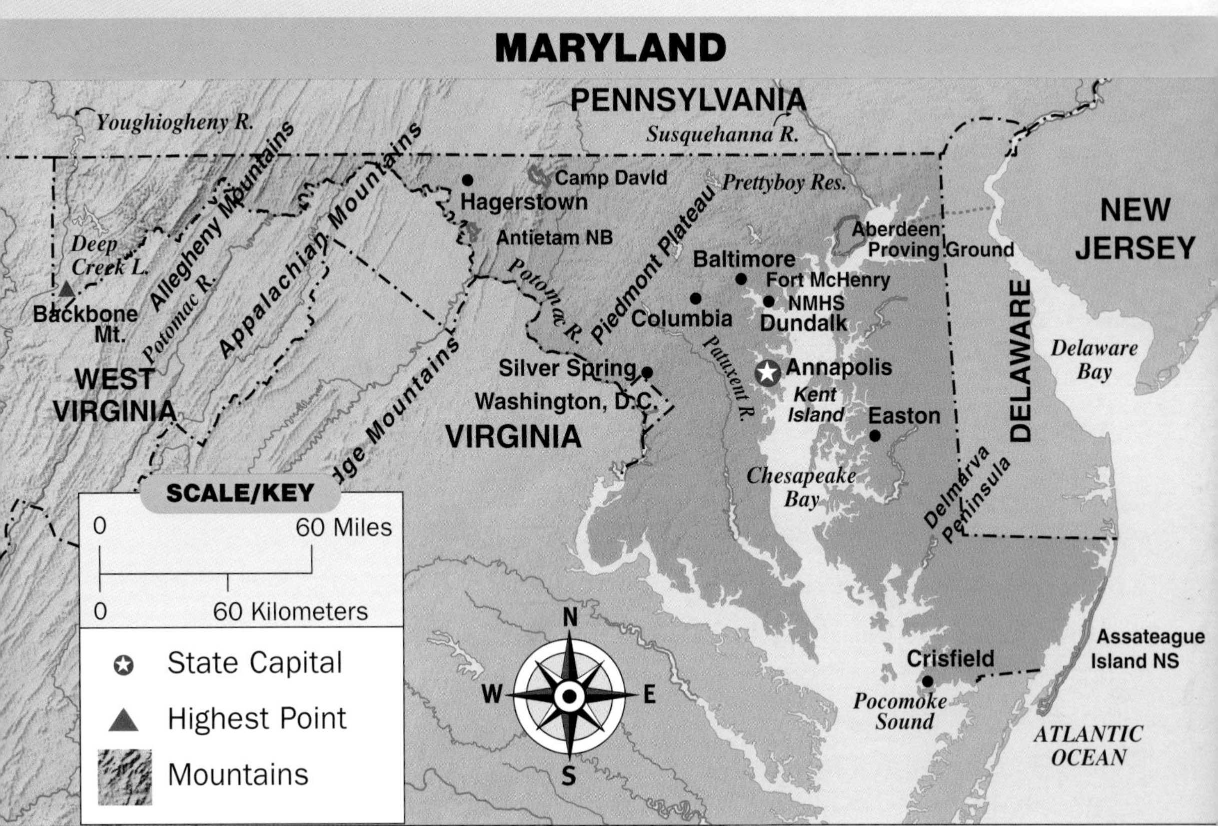

The Chesapeake Bay cuts deep into Maryland from the ocean. The bay has a ragged coastline and many islands. Clams, crabs, oysters, and other shellfish live in the chilly water.

The Susquehanna River is the largest river in Maryland. Like most rivers in the state, it flows into the Chesapeake. The Potomac River forms much of Maryland's western border. A number of smaller rivers flow through the state, too. Trout, catfish, and carp swim in many of the rivers and streams.

The Coastal Plain

The land around the Chesapeake is part of the Atlantic Coastal Plain. This plain covers about one-half of the state. The soil in the north is very rich. It is good for growing crops. Farther south, the soil is sandy.

The Eastern Shore is flat and low. Salt marshes cover some of the land. Grassy plants known as sedges grow in the marshes, and ducks and geese build nests here.

Major Rivers

Susquehanna River
444 miles (714 km) long

Potomac River
287 miles (462 km) long

Youghiogheny River
150 miles (240 km) long

In the south, pine trees grow in forests. The woods make good homes for squirrels, deer, and opossums.

The Western Shore has flat land and low hills. Cliffs

The Piedmont has some of the best farmland in Maryland. The hills are gentle here and the soil is very rich.

drop down to the bay. The black-eyed Susan grows here. It is the state flower. Berries attract animals and birds. The Baltimore oriole, the state bird, is a common sight here. Rabbits, minks, foxes, and chipmunks live in this area, too.

The Piedmont

The Piedmont **Plateau** lies farther west. It is about 40 miles (64 km) wide. The land is higher here. It is made up of rolling hills and valleys. Raccoons, rabbits, deer, and foxes are just a few of the animals that live here. The area's rich soil is good for farming.

Camp David

Camp David is in the Blue Ridge Mountains. Since 1945, Camp David has been the official **retreat** of U.S. presidents. The camp has rooms for the president and others to eat, sleep, and talk. Many presidents have used Camp David. They relax, enjoy nature, and meet with special guests there.

Mountains

Three mountain ranges lie west of the Piedmont. They are the Appalachian, Blue Ridge, and Allegheny Mountains. The state's highest point is Backbone Mountain. It is 3,360 feet (1,024 meters) high.

The mountains are the coolest part of the state. Pine, spruce, beech, maple, and oak trees grow on the slopes. Many small animals live here, along with a few bears and bobcats. Wild turkeys and quail also live in this part of the state.

Economy

Part of the state of Maryland is next to Washington, D.C. Washington is the U.S. capital. Because Maryland is close by, many military bases have been built in this state. Big **federal** offices have been built here, too. All of these places provide jobs for people in Maryland.

In this state, more people have service jobs than any other kind of job. People who work in service jobs help others. Government workers have service jobs. People who work in tourism have service jobs, too. Many tourists visit Maryland. They go to the beach at Ocean City and visit the harbor in Baltimore. They stay in

The beach at Ocean City draws millions of tourists every summer.

hotels and eat in restaurants. These kinds of places need many workers to serve all of the tourists.

Factories, Farms, and Fish

Factories also provide jobs in the state. Some factories make chemicals and food products. Some print books and magazines. Goods made here are sold all over the world.

Farmland covers about one-third of the state. Milk products and chickens are the top farm products. Many farmers grow plants and trees for sale. Some grow soybeans, tobacco, corn and other crops.

Fishing is a big business on the Chesapeake Bay. The bay has become **polluted**, however. This has been bad for the fish. Now, the state's government is working to clean up the water.

How Money Is Made in Maryland

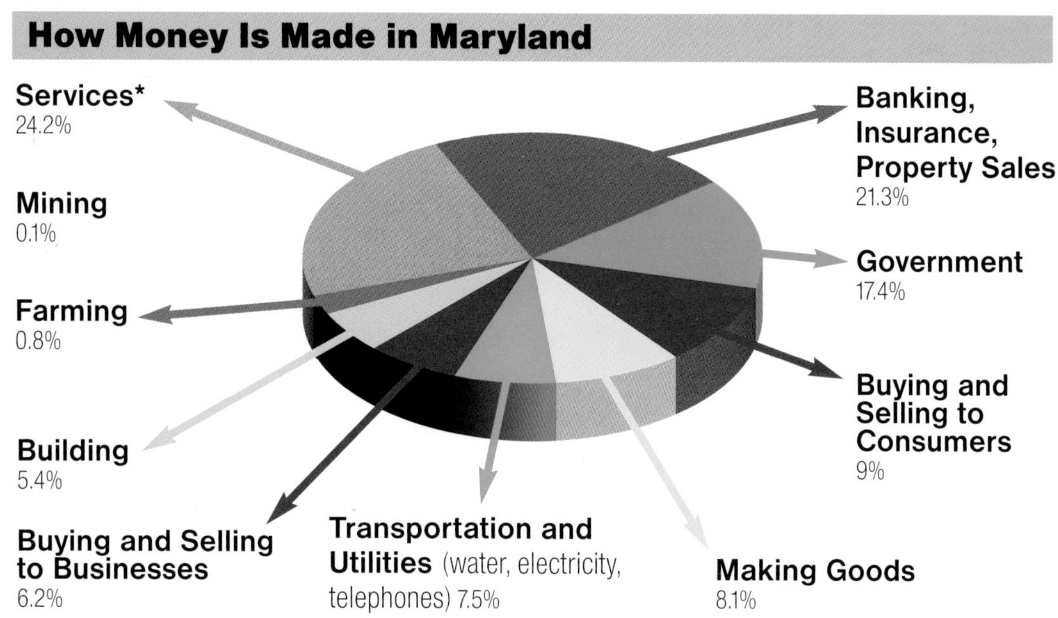

* Services include jobs in hotels, restaurants, auto repair, medicine, teaching, and entertainment.

Government

Annapolis is the capital of Maryland. The leaders of the state work there. The state government has three parts. They are the executive, legislative, and judicial branches.

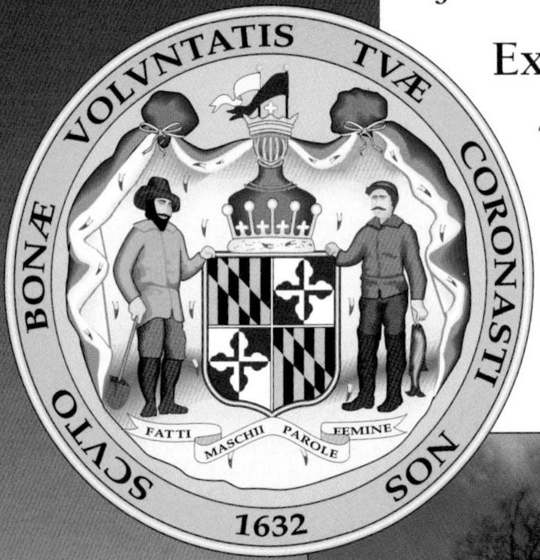

Executive Branch

The executive branch carries out the laws of the state. The governor is head of this branch. The lieutenant governor helps the governor.

The State House is in Annapolis. It has been used as a state capitol longer than any other building in the country.

The governor of Maryland lives in the Government House in Annapolis. This huge house has been used by the state's governors for more than 125 years.

Legislative Branch

The legislative branch makes the laws for the state. The Maryland legislature is called the General Assembly. It has two parts. The parts are the Senate and the House of Delegates. These two groups work together to make laws.

Judicial Branch

Judges and courts make up the judicial branch. They may decide whether people who have been **accused of** committing crimes are guilty.

Local Governments

Maryland has twenty-three counties. Most counties are run by a small group of people. Most cities are led by a mayor and city council.

MARYLAND'S STATE GOVERNMENT

Executive

Office	Length of Term
Governor	4 years
Lieutenant Governor	4 years

Legislative

Body	Length of Term
Senate (47 members)	4 years
House of Delegates (141 members)	4 years

Judicial

Court	Length of Term
Appeals (7 judges)	10 years
Special Appeals (13 judges)	10 years

Things to See and Do

Maryland is a great place to enjoy the outdoors. You can sail on the Chesapeake Bay. You can ski or hike in the western mountains. You can go to the coast and spend a day at the beach.

Maryland has dozens of state parks. At Rocks State Park, **boulders** are piled on top of each other in odd ways. At Calvert Cliffs State Park, visitors find **fossils** on the beach. Susquehanna State Park has great bike trails.

Around the Chesapeake Bay, many wildlife areas have been created. One of them is at Ellis Bay. It is a fine place for

Windsurfers catch a brisk breeze on the Chesapeake Bay.

bird watching, deer hunting, and fishing.

Historic Sites and Museums

Historic sites and museums are found all over the state. Fort Frederick is close to Hagerstown. It was built in the 1700s. The Antietam National Battlefield is not far away. A terrible Civil War battle took place at this site. Baltimore is home to the Maryland Historical Society. There you can see the page on which Francis Scott Key wrote "The Star-Spangled Banner." In Annapolis, you can go to the U.S. Naval Academy Museum. It has displays of old swords and uniforms, model ships, and more.

Sports and Festivals

Baltimore is a great place for sports lovers.

Indoor Fun

If you like fish, head for the National Aquarium in Baltimore. You can see dolphins, sharks, rays, and all kinds of tropical fish. If you are interested in space travel, go to the Goddard Space Flight Center in Greenbelt. You may get to see a model rocket launch.

The National Aquarium is in Baltimore. It is one of the best aquariums in the country. You can see thousands of fish and watch trained dolphins do tricks in return for tasty bits of fish.

Famous People of Maryland

Frederick Douglass

Born: About February 1817, Tuckahoe, Maryland

Died: February 20, 1895, Washington, D.C.

Frederick Douglass was born a slave. When he was young, he was sent to Baltimore to work. In 1838, he ran away from his master and made his way north. He began speaking out about the evils of slavery. Later, he wrote a book about his life as a slave. He also published a newspaper for people who **opposed** slavery. Douglass became a famous leader who worked for equal rights for all.

Football fans cheer for the Baltimore Ravens. They won the Super Bowl in 2001. Baseball fans go to Oriole Park at Camden Yards to watch the Baltimore Orioles play their home games. Fans of horse racing enjoy the Preakness Stakes. This is one of the top **thoroughbred** races of the year.

They're off! The crowd roars as some of the fastest horses in the country run the Preakness Stakes race in 2005.

Famous People of Maryland

"Babe" Ruth

Born: February 6, 1895, Baltimore, Maryland

Died: August 16, 1948, New York, New York

Babe Ruth was one of the greatest baseball players ever. He was born George Herman Ruth. His family was poor, and he often roamed the streets. He learned to play baseball at a school for troubled boys. Ruth grew up to become one of the most famous players in baseball. He played for the Boston Red Sox and the New York Yankees. In 1927, he became the first player in the major leagues to hit sixty home runs in one season. Baltimore is home to the Babe Ruth Birthplace and Museum. It is a great place to learn more about "the Babe."

Festivals are held here all year long. The National Hard Crab Derby is held in Crisfield. It features crab races, a crab-picking contest, and a parade. Sandy Spring holds its Strawberry Festival in June. Easton holds a Waterfowl Festival every fall.

George Herman Ruth was known to baseball fans as "The Babe." This great hitter became one of the first members of the Baseball Hall of Fame.

GLOSSARY

accused of — blamed for

boulders — huge rocks

civil rights — basic rights of all people to be treated equally under the law

colony — a group of people living in a new land but keeping ties with the place they came from

federal — having to do with national government

fossils — parts of plants or the bones and shells of animals that hardened into rock over thousands of years

Great Depression — a time, in the 1930s, when many people lost jobs and businesses lost money

immigrants — people who leave one country to live in another country

opposed — were against

plateau — a large area of flat land that is higher than the land around it

polluted — poisoned

protest — to speak out against something

race riots — wild actions by crowds of people who are angry at people of another race

retreat — a quiet, safe place where people can get away from everyday life

survey — to measure land

thoroughbred — a type of racehorse that is bred for lightness and speed, or an animal that is a pure breed

Union — the states that stayed loyal to the federal government during the U.S. Civil War; the North

TO FIND OUT MORE

Books

Awesome Chesapeake: A Kid's Guide to the Bay. David Owen Bell (Tidewater)

B Is for Blue Crab: A Maryland Alphabet. Discover America State By State (series). Shirley Menendez (Sleeping Bear Press)

The Colony of Maryland. The Thirteen Colonies and the Lost Colony (series). Brooke Coleman (PowerKids Press)

Escape North! The Story of Harriet Tubman. Step-Into-Reading (series). Monica Kulling (Random House Books for Young Readers)

Maryland: The History of Maryland Colony, 1634-1776. 13 Colonies (series). Roberta Wiener (Raintree)

Web Sites

Enchanted Learning: Maryland
www.enchantedlearning.com/usa/states/maryland/

Fort McHenry
www.bcpl.net/~etowner/patriots.html

Time Tunnel
www.dnr.state.md.us/programs/timetunnel/timetunnel.html

Sea Turtles of Maryland
www.dnr.state.md.us/wildlife/turtles.asp

INDEX